A Kid's Guide to
GENEALOGY

BASIC
GENEALOGY
FOR KIDS

Bonnie Hinman

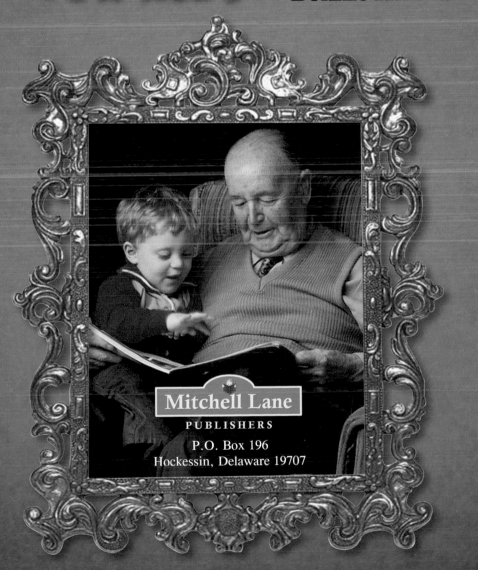

Mitchell Lane
PUBLISHERS

P.O. Box 196
Hockessin, Delaware 19707

Mitchell Lane
PUBLISHERS

Basic Genealogy for Kids
How to Research Your Ancestry
Using Technology to Find Your Family History
Design Your Family Tree

Copyright © 2012 by Mitchell Lane Publishers

All rights reserved. No part of this book may be reproduced without written permission from the publisher. Printed and bound in the United States of America.

PUBLISHER'S NOTE: The facts on which the story in this book is based have been thoroughly researched. Documentation of such research can be found on page 44. While every possible effort has been made to ensure accuracy, the publisher will not assume liability for damages caused by inaccuracies in the data, and makes no warranty on the accuracy of the information contained herein.

The Internet sites referenced herein were active as of the publication date. Due to the fleeting nature of some web sites, we cannot guarantee that they will all be active when you are reading this book.

Printing		2	3	4	5	6	7	8	9

**Library of Congress
Cataloging-in-Publication Data**
Hinman, Bonnie.
Basic genealogy for kids / by Bonnie Hinman.
  p. cm.—(A kid's guide to genealogy)
Includes bibliographical references and index.
ISBN 978-1-58415-949-0 (library bound)
1. Genealogy—Juvenile literature. I. Title.
CS15.5.H56 2011
929'.1—dc22

4622   2011000616

eBook ISBN: 9781612280929

PLB/PLB2

Contents

INTRODUCTION: CLIMBING THE FAMILY TREE

When my husband began researching his family tree, he became absorbed in finding out who Sarah Sally Blake was, and whether she married his distant ancestor. I was interested but found it hard to keep all of his relatives straight. And I suspected that Sarah Sally was not a real name, since Sally is often used as a nickname for Sarah.

A few months after he began looking for his ancestors, he announced that he was going to look for mine. As it turned out, both sides of my family were easy to find using online sources. My maiden name is Wirts, and as expected, my ancestors came from Germany. They had immigrated to the United States in the early 1700s. I was impressed.

It was my mother's family name, Bright, that held the first surprise. I had always assumed that Bright was a solid English name. In fact, my mother's family name started out as Breicht and changed over several decades to Bright. Breicht is a German

name, and sure enough my ancestors had come from Germany. They too had arrived in the United States in the 1700s.

The biggest surprise of all was that both branches of my family had settled in Pennsylvania. They could have known each other in those early days much sooner than when my parents met in Southwest Missouri in the 1940s. One of my ancestors founded a Moravian church. One ancestor helped supply Revolutionary War troops with food, which makes me eligible to join the Daughters of the American Revolution. Who knew?

I have a little more respect these days when my husband mumbles about his research. He's still trying to prove that Sarah Sally Blake was his ancestor. He knows that Sarah Sally existed but can't prove it with a census or other document. She wasn't anyone famous, but he is determined to claim Sarah Sally as an official ancestor. I look over his shoulder once in a while and sometimes offer my very German skills to help him. His search continues.

Family meals are a great time to talk about the good old days.

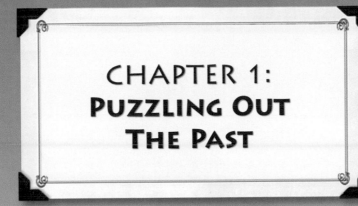

CHAPTER 1: PUZZLING OUT THE PAST

When families get together for Thanksgiving, weddings, or other celebrations, they often talk about days past. Sometimes they call it "the good old days." Just when you're wondering how they can have been "good old days" if there were no video games, you hear something interesting. You perk up your ears, quit chewing pumpkin pie, and listen more closely.

Perhaps your great-uncle Henry says to your grandmother, "What have you heard about old Homer lately?"

"He sent a letter to Ida that said he was writing songs for some big country star," Grandma said, "but I don't believe a word of it."

"He always was a big talker. Didn't he say that his grandfather was a hero in the Spanish-American War?"

"Yeah," Grandma says, "but I'm not so sure about that. His grandfather couldn't have been very old then. I doubt that old Sylvester, that was his name, ever fought with Teddy Roosevelt like Homer says. And I'd be even more surprised if Sylvester was some kind of war hero."

The discussion about good-for-nothing Homer continues, but you find yourself thinking. Maybe great-great-uncle Homer's grandfather really was with Teddy Roosevelt in Cuba during the Spanish-American War. It

Theodore "Teddy" Roosevelt and his Rough Riders captured San Juan Hill in Cuba during the Spanish-American War of 1898. Could one of your ancestors have been there with him?

would be great to have a real hero in the family. How could you find out if what Homer says is true?

You have a puzzle to solve. Solving puzzles is a big part of researching a family tree. Today that kind of research is called genealogy (jee-nee-AL-uh-jee)—the study of family lines of descent. It is the story of the family members who lived before you. The story winds back through your parents and then your grandparents and great-grandparents and so on until there are too many "greats" to fit on the page. There will also be a whole lot of cousins, aunts, and uncles.

Genealogy is the story of where your family members were born and when, where they lived, whom they married, how many children they had, and when they died. Along the way it may be possible to find out how they lived and what kind of people they were.

Playing detective to find out your family history is fun, but there are other reasons to research your ancestors. The word *genealogy* means "study of genes." Genes are tiny units in our body cells that are responsible for inherited traits—the ways in which we are like our parents, grandparents, or other ancestors. Your genes determine or influence physical traits such as height, weight, hair color, and eye color. They also play a role in whether you will have certain strengths or interests.

Some traits are dominant and others are recessive. For example, brown eyes are a dominant trait. A person with brown eyes will either have two genes for brown eyes, or one gene for brown eyes and one gene for another color. The other color is the recessive trait. If two parents have the genes for brown eyes, with no recessive genes, their child will have brown eyes. If one parent has brown eyes and the other has blue with no recessive genes, that child will have brown eyes. If one parent has blue eyes and the other has brown eyes with a recessive blue gene, the child might have blue or brown eyes.

This explanation is simple, and for a long time scientists believed it was complete. They now know that there may be many more genes that determine eye color.[1] Even so, following eye color through your family tree can be a fun project.

Male pattern baldness is also determined by genetics. For a long time people believed this trait was inherited from the mother's side of the family. Research in the early 2000s shows that the baldness gene is on the X chromosome, which men get from their mother—proving the theory to be true.[2]

Color blindness is also inherited from the mother. It is more common in males because of the way the chromosomes are inherited. Dominant and recessive genes are at work again in determining red hair. The ways in which the genes are combined may make a trait like red hair seem to skip a generation. It could come from an aunt or uncle, as has been commonly believed, and a red-haired parent may or may not have a redheaded child.

If something goes wrong in a gene, it can cause a disease or disorder in your body. These disorders and diseases can be inherited if the abnormal gene is transmitted to a descendant. Sometimes it is helpful to research the family tree to see if other family members had the same problem. Some diseases that can be inherited are cystic fibrosis, sickle cell anemia, and Tay Sachs disease. Genetics is a complicated science. Just because a parent or other ancestor has a genetic disease does not mean that a child will inherit that gene.

There are other genetic reasons to discover your ancestors that are not as serious. It can be fun to see if someone else had your

Are you the only one in your family with red hair who likes to play the piano? If you research your ancestors, you may find a dance-hall piano player or a piano maker. Their hair may have been red just like yours.

Famous German scientist Albert Einstein immigrated to America in 1933. He received his certificate of U.S. citizenship from Judge Phillip Forman in 1940. If you are good at math or science, perhaps one of your ancestors was a famous scientist like Einstein.

red hair or loved music like you do. Were any ancestors scientists like you want to be? Were any ancestors actors like your little sister wants to be?

One popular reason to research your family tree is to see if any of your ancestors were famous. An ancestor is someone who lived before you with the same bloodline. You have to be directly descended for a relative to be your ancestor. (Your aunts, uncles, and cousins are related to you, but they are not your ancestors.) Did one of your ancestors really come to North America on the *Mayflower* with the Pilgrims like your great-great aunt Ethel said? It's possible.

Do you know anyone who says George Washington was his or her ancestor? You'll know they are teasing, because George Washington didn't have any children of his own. His wife, Martha, had children from a first marriage, so Martha Washington could be your ancestor.

Old pictures can tell many stories about our ancestors. Perhaps your mother still has a piece of jewelry that her great-grandmother wore.

Sometimes the discovery of an old family photograph album, letters, or other old family possession can make you wonder who those people were. Perhaps you found a very old picture labeled Uncle Steve. Was this the Uncle Steve that your great-great grandmother said fought in the Civil War? Your grandmother said he never married. So who is the woman in the picture with him?

Genealogy research can answer most of these questions, but you'll have to play detective to find the right pieces to complete the puzzle of Uncle Steve or Uncle Sylvester. A detective uses many tools and methods for tracking down the facts of a case. A genealogy detective also has a slew of tools and methods for solving the puzzles of his or her family history.

Remember that genealogy is history. The ancestors who populate your family tree were real people. Be as careful and as accurate as possible when you record facts about those people. Check and double-check your research.

The Maori Indians of New Zealand memorized their genealogy. They decorated their faces with moko to show importance within the tribe and to be attractive to the opposite gender.

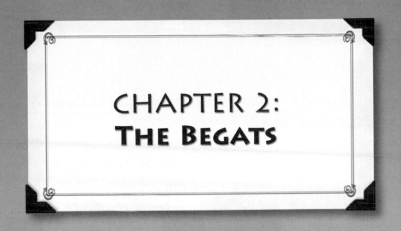

CHAPTER 2:
THE BEGATS

Who inherits money and land? Who gets to be king or chief or ruler next? To answer these questions, ancient peoples kept track of family lines of descent. Genealogy wasn't a hobby for them—a person's family history could be a matter of life or death. Until the twentieth century, almost all cultures declared that the oldest son would inherit his father's property and position upon the father's death. This is called patrilineal descent. In some cultures, inheritance was passed through the mother, and this is called matrilineal descent.

Patrilineal descent worked well enough unless a father did not have any living sons. Then land or other property had to jump to a different branch of the family tree. A nephew or cousin might be named heir. Perhaps two cousins both claimed to be the heir. Wars were fought over such claims. Kingdoms needed accurate records of birth and death dates to help resolve these conflicts.

Each culture developed its own way of keeping track of these important dates. Many early genealogies were not written. In a tribe or culture without a written language, a tribal historian would memorize the records, then pass them along orally. The Maori people of New Zealand kept track of generations this way, and they still do. One early twentieth-century

Maori chieftain recited a 34-generation history of his people. He named more than 700 family members to a researcher.[1]

Somewhere between oral and written genealogical records are totem poles. The northwest coastal Indians such as Haida and Tlingit carved symbols on the tall wooden poles. The symbols were memory devices to help the groups remember their history and genealogy.

The Egyptians and Chinese were among the first ancient peoples to keep written records of ancestry. Both cultures were ruled by lines of royal families called dynasties. Power and great wealth were passed down from generation to generation. The lower-class Chinese also kept family records. Even the poorest home had an altar with the names of ancestors.

The ancient Greeks and Romans mixed up their family trees with the genealogy of the gods they worshiped. Many rulers claimed to be related to one or more of the gods, and they showed it using family trees. As a descendant of a god, the ruler showed his right to authority.

The Bible is full of genealogical information. Some chapters are called the begat chapters because they are long lists of Jesse begat (fathered) David and David begat Solomon and so on. The genealogies were important to the ancient Hebrews to prove descent for the priesthood, as well as for rule and inheritance.

Emperor Haile Selassie of Ethiopia claimed that he was the 225th ruler of the hereditary line that began when King Solomon married the Queen of Sheba. Genealogical researcher Robert Gunderson says that it isn't possible to trace a family with accuracy much farther back than 450 CE.[2] Earlier records are unreliable and often tangled with myth and legend. This doesn't mean that Emperor Selassie wasn't related to King Solomon, but it does mean that he'd have a hard time proving it with certainty.

In England the earliest written record of land ownership was the Domesday Book. In 1066, William the Conqueror invaded and conquered England. He awarded property to his loyal followers, and in 1085 while ruling as William I, he decided to conduct a survey of his territory. He sent men throughout England to find out who owned what land and how many cows, oxen, and other assets each landowner claimed. The results were recorded in the Domesday Book. King William had a large army to maintain, and he wanted to check his subjects to see how much tax they could afford to pay him.

The Domesday Book got its name when people realized that if their name wasn't on the list, they would lose legal rights to their property. The book doomed them to become landless English subjects. If your name was on the list, you were a member of the early English upper class. People could point with pride to the fact that an ancestor's name had been in the Domesday Book. The document still exists. It is kept in the British National Archives in London.

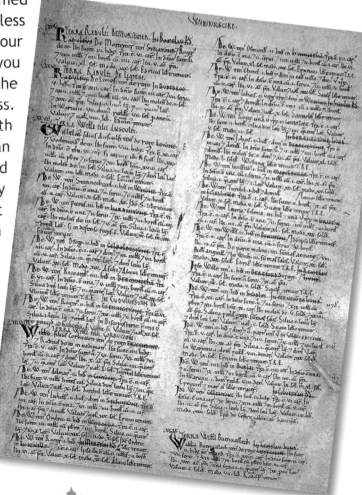

The Domesday book was handwritten in the 11th century. This page includes listings for Birmingham of Warwickshire in England.

The Pilgrims wrote the Mayflower Compact while still on board their ship on November 11, 1620. The Compact described how the Pilgrims would govern themselves in America.

In the United States, people did not commonly search for famous ancestors until after the American Revolution. Before then they were too busy staying alive while building a new country. After the Revolution, some wealthier Americans looked for other ways besides how much money they had to show that their families were special. It was popular to be able to say that you were related to one of the "first families of Virginia" or that you had an ancestor who arrived on the *Mayflower* in 1620. It was also an honor to be related to someone who signed the Declaration of Independence or fought in the American Revolution.

An important genealogy association called the Daughters of the American Revolution (DAR) was started in 1890. The DAR accepts women for membership who can prove descent from anyone who helped America gain independence. This group is not just for descendants of soldiers who fought in the Revolutionary War, as is often thought. Doctors, ministers, state officials, or those who furnished supplies to the Continental army are only a few of the kinds of ancestors who would make a woman eligible to join the DAR. The DAR was founded when women were excluded from men's societies, such as the Sons of the American Revolution (SAR).

This era saw the beginning of quite a bit of "fuzzy" genealogy. Genealogy researchers popped up to help wealthy families prove their ancestral claims. Some researchers were honest, but many told their customers what they wanted to hear without backing the claim with reliable sources. A great many people were delighted to find out that they were the lost heirs of an English duke. They didn't really want to hear the truth—that their great-great-uncle had been a baker in the poor district of London.

While many people were interested in family trees in the eighteenth and nineteenth centuries, two events happened in the 1970s that spiked intense interest in genealogy. The first was the celebration of the 200th anniversary of the signing of the Declaration of Independence. The 1976 Bicentennial made

Store windows in Philadelphia during the summer of 1976 were filled with souvenirs to celebrate America's 200th birthday.

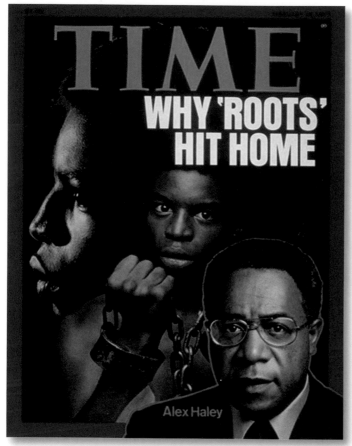

Time **magazine cover, 1977**

Americans think about the early days of the country. Towns all across the United States held parties in honor of America's birthday.

At nearly the same time as the Bicentennial, a book called *Roots: The Saga of an American Family* was published. Written by Alex Haley, *Roots* was the story of Haley's African ancestor Kunte Kinte and how he came to America. Kinte was captured in Gambia in 1767, brought to the United States, and sold into slavery. The story continues through several generations of Kunte Kinte's descendants.

In 1977 the book was made into a television miniseries, which attracted a huge audience of 133 million viewers. The series won nine Emmy awards and was one of the most-watched television programs in history. The Bicentennial and *Roots* seemed to wake Americans up to the history we all share, as well as to the roots we have individually.

All Americans except Native Americans are descended from immigrants from other countries. If you have an Irish background and discover that your ancestors came to the United States

Be suspicious of claims that a family is descended from someone famous. Being descended from an Indian princess is not possible because there were no such things as Indian princesses. Stories passed down from generation to generation often change in the retelling, so check what you hear against official records.

between 1845 and 1852, they probably left Ireland during the Great Potato Famine. A deadly fungus called potato blight destroyed the potato crop for several years there. Rural families depended on potatoes for food. To survive, over a million Irish people immigrated to the United States.

Many Chinese immigrants arrived in the 1860s to work on the Transcontinental Railroad, which was completed in 1869. A decade later, more Irish immigrated to work on building the Brooklyn Bridge in New York City. In the 1930s and 1940s, German and Eastern European Jews came to America to escape the persecution that Adolf Hitler inflicted on them. These and many other events drove people to undertake the daring journey to a new land.

After 1892, millions of immigrants, mostly from Eastern Europe and the Middle East, passed through Ellis Island, a government immigration center located in New York Harbor. The new arrivals were processed and checked for disease before being taken by ferry across the harbor to New York City. Close to 40 percent of all current U.S. citizens can trace at least one of their ancestors to Ellis Island.[3]

The first step in researching your family tree is to ask your parents what they remember about older relatives. Take notes about or video-record what they tell you.

CHAPTER 3: FINDING THE FIRST CLUES

It may seem overwhelming to start researching your family history. What do you do first to find out if your great-great-uncle fought with Teddy Roosevelt in the Spanish-American War? Do you look up the war or Teddy Roosevelt or the U.S. Army?

Finding the first clues is usually the easiest part of family tree research. You ask your parents to tell you all they remember about older relatives. They might remember only the names, but they could know many details about them. There are three important dates that genealogists value when researching a person for a family history: the date of birth, date of marriage, and date of death. Knowing where the family lived can also be a helpful clue. Keep track of names and relationships as you get more information.

As you gather names, fill out a family tree form. Some baby books have family tree forms that look like real trees. You can also download many different forms for recording family relationships. Don't forget that you are working backward in time to find out more about your ancestors. If you use a branching form that reads from left to right (it looks like a bracket drawing for a sports tournament), you will have many more entries on the left side of the form.

Talk to grandparents or great-grandparents about their memories. Sometimes one person in an extended family will serve as an unofficial historian for that family. That person will have plenty to tell you about the family history.

Family reunions are a great place to work on your family tree. Part of the fun of family reunions is talking about past events. One relative's story helps another relative remember something else, which in turn sparks another memory. Details will pile up as you listen to the talk. Take notes at these gatherings.

Holidays and other family celebrations are other times to see what older members of your family remember about their lives. Each time you ask a question, a relative may remember another story or detail that can help you fill in your family tree. Collect these stories if you can, but concentrate on location and the three big dates—birth, marriage, and death.

Family reunions are fun for everyone. You may find out that you have much in common with distant cousins, aunts, and uncles, including a crazy sense of humor.

What do you do if you live far from any of your relatives and don't attend family reunions? Sometimes parents divorce and a child may not be in touch with one or the other branch of the family. These situations make it harder but not impossible to research your family history.

Adopted children sometimes know or find out their biological parents' names and research blood relatives. However, an adopted child is just as much a member of his or her adopted family as he or she would be as a birth child. Researching the family tree you have joined can be done the same way and may reveal more interesting results than if you had researched your birth family.

E-mails, letters, and social web sites are some of the best ways to overcome distance. Start with what you know and contact distant relatives about your family history. Some are bound to respond with clues that will help your research. If you don't have any addresses, it may be possible to get phone numbers and then addresses from phonebooks and other records. If one branch of the family seems to have led to a dead end, switch to a different branch to research.

If you find yourself absolutely stumped with all of your family lines, ask your parents if you can hire a professional genealogist to attack the problem. A few are listed on page 45. They can help you decide when to hire a professional and how much it might cost.[1]

Genealogists often talk about generations. You are the first generation in your family, your parents are the second generation, your grandparents are the third generation, and your great-grandparents are the fourth, and so on. Since it takes two people to make a child, you have two parents, four grandparents, eight great-grandparents, and sixteen great-great-grandparents. If you went back ten generations in your family, you would have over 2,000 blood relatives.

Your ancestors may seem gone, but they are always over your shoulder.

That's a lot of branches on the family tree. Be sure to keep names and dates straight when you switch from one generation to another because it is easy to get confused. This kind of chart of parents and grandparents doesn't even mention all the aunts, uncles, and cousins that also populate the family tree.

Another place to start can be in a cemetery. Some relatives are buried in old family cemeteries, or in the same part of a bigger cemetery. Big cemeteries often have logbooks in which grave locations are recorded. Once you find the grave, the headstone or marker usually tells the name, birth date, and death date of the person buried there.

You can record this information in different ways. Of course you can simply make a list with the information, or you might take a picture of the marker. Another interesting way to record the marker's words is by doing a tracing or rubbing. First, tape a piece of white paper over the words on the marker and then use charcoal or a pencil to rub over the paper. The image of the words on the marker will show up on the paper.

Once you have names and dates, you are ready to look for other clues in your search to discover your family history.

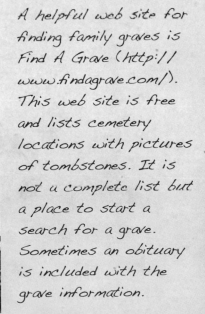

A helpful web site for finding family graves is Find A Grave (http://www.findagrave.com/). This web site is free and lists cemetery locations with pictures of tombstones. It is not a complete list but a place to start a search for a grave. Sometimes an obituary is included with the grave information.

A man who lived in this type of house in England might have been called Henry of the Hills. Last names, also called surnames, were not officially required in England until after William the Conqueror became king.

CHAPTER 4:
DIGGING DEEPER

As you follow your family tree back through the generations, you might notice that the names get tricky. You can't be certain that the last name or surname that your family has now is the same one that your great great-great-grandfather had.

Last names did not exist in many cultures. They weren't needed when everyone knew everyone else in a village or town. Kings and emperors and other rulers started the naming game. They realized that in order to tax their people, they needed a way to keep track of who lived where and owned what. An English village in the 1200s might have several men named William or Henry. The village people used the men's first names plus a description of the work they did, where they lived, or how they looked. For example, there was William who lived in the meadows; William the cooper (barrel maker); Henry who was very short; and Henry who lived on the hill.

When the king's men arrived to count people, they were confused by who was who. For the king's convenience, the village Williams and Henrys became William Meadows, William Cooper, Henry Short, and Henry Hill. It was a simple solution and worked well.

English and other European surnames come almost entirely from four categories: occupations, parents' names, places, and descriptions. Smith is the most common last name in the United States. Metal smiths such as blacksmiths and silversmiths were plentiful and important in villages and towns when last names were first recorded, so many people had Smith as a last name.

There were many Johns, so "son of John"—Johnson—was popular as well. "Son of William" was also common as Williamson, which could be shortened as Williams. *Mc* and *Mac* also mean "son of," so MacDonald means "son of Donald."

Place names are by far the largest source of last names. They include such names as Hill, Atwater, Rivers, Marsh, and Wood. Some last names described the person's looks or personality, such as Short, Longfellow, Brown, Sweet, and Merriman. Some names are combinations. The ending -*kin* means "little," so "little William" would be Wilkin, and his son would be Wilkinson or Wilkins.

The problem for a family tree is that these names often changed over many years. Spelling wasn't standard even among educated people of long ago. Most people couldn't read or write, so they didn't know how their names were supposed to be spelled. And Smith in other languages might be spelled Smythe, Smyth, Smithe, or even Schmitt.

There were people who changed their names on purpose. Some Europeans who came to America wanted to Americanize their names. Bleu became Blue, while Noblinski became Noble. These changes might have happened by accident, too. Immigration officials didn't always understand or know how to spell the immigrants' real names.

It was also common for grown children of immigrants to change their names so that they might better fit into their new country. Fitzgeral became Fitzgerald. St. Claire became Sinclair. There were also family naming patterns and religious customs that affected last names. Some religious groups name children for dead relatives. Families might name the first male in every family Henry or James, which led to a whole lot of cousins with the same first

Immigrant children who arrived at Ellis Island were carefully checked for sickness or disease. If found to be ill, a child twelve years old or older could be sent back to Europe alone. Younger children had to have a parent go with them. Many families were split up this way.

and last name. A few last names came from the mother's name, although this tradition was much less common. Anson (son of Ann) and Nelson (son of Nell) are examples.

People who were brought from Africa and sold as slaves were often given the last name of their owners. It wasn't until the census of 1870 that former slaves were listed by name. Before the Civil War they were entered as a number under their owner's name. This practice makes it harder to trace black ancestors before the Civil War.

Many immigrants from Asia during the nineteenth and twentieth centuries also changed their names. Chinese and Vietnamese are tonal languages, meaning that the same word may have several different meanings depending upon the way it is pronounced. Americans found the Asian names hard to pronounce correctly, so the immigrants often changed their first or last name, or both, to more American-sounding names.

You can use computers to research your family tree. Many documents have been digitized and made available on the Internet. More are added every day.

Knowing that names can change, where does a genealogist start to research his or her family tree? As you search back through the generations, don't assume that a last name spelled differently from yours isn't a relative. English names were changed the least, but you may find that the English-sounding name Bright mentioned before was changed from Breicht, which is solidly German.

There are many written sources to help you in your search for ancestors. A few of them are census records, city directories, newspaper obituaries, military records, county histories, and school records. Libraries, courthouses, and the Internet are the best places to start the search for written records.

Official U.S. Census recordkeeping began in 1790 when the residents of the former thirteen colonies and their adjoining territories were counted. After 1790, the census was taken every ten years. Some colonies counted from about 1600 on, but these records are incomplete. Even the 1790 federal census has many gaps and errors. Several states' records were destroyed in a fire in Washington, D.C., when the British burned the capital during the War of 1812.

Before the 1850 census, only heads of households were listed by name. Women and children were listed by sex and age only. In 1850 this changed to include the name, exact age, occupation, and place of birth of each household resident.

For privacy reasons, the U.S. government does not release entire census year information until 72 years after it is collected. For example, the 1940 census would not be released to the public until 2012. Previous censuses are available for anyone

A census taker canvasses a neighborhood in Lincoln, Nebraska, in 1910.

to view. Microfilm of the original documents can be borrowed from the National Archives. Some censuses have been digitized and are available online, but most of these sites require that you become a member by paying a fee. Occasionally a large library will provide the online service for free. Even with these obstacles, census records remain the easiest and most valuable source for family tree research.[1]

Libraries often keep old city directories, which can be a great source if you know the span of years and name for your relative. County histories may be helpful, although most aren't indexed. The library may also have old newspaper obituaries in its files, or the librarian may be able to order them.

At the county courthouse, you can find probate and court records and published deeds to property. Military records showing

Librarians are excellent helpers when you research your family tree. They will be happy to assist you in finding the materials you need.

enlistment and discharge details may also be found at the courthouse. More complete military records can be found in the National Archives in Washington, D.C., and at the National Military Personnel Records Center in St. Louis, Missouri.

School records are sometimes available from the school if the request is for an old record. If the school no longer exists, the county department of education may have some information.

Museums may also maintain collections of old photographs and other artifacts. Some photos may have been indexed and could provide clues for your search. Donors of artifacts are often profiled briefly with the things they gave the museum. You may discover that your great-great-grandfather collected pistols and donated his collection to the museum.

The Internet has emerged as the single best road to researching your family history, and it can provide much of the information that you may be able to find at any of the above places. However, the Internet may not be as much fun to use as visiting cemeteries, museums, libraries, and courthouses, and it may not be as reliable as original sources.

The head of household listed in the census records isn't always the father. It could be a widowed mother, relative, guardian, or other person. If both mother and father are listed as heads of separate households, they may have been divorced.

Gradually a family tree researcher builds up a mountain of information about his or her family. The next challenge is how to find your great-great-uncle's birth date in the piles of paper and computer files that you have collected. The information has to be sorted and organized. That is a job in itself.

Old pictures can be the key to finding out more information about your ancestors. The photos may sometimes jog a relative's memory to recall stories about other family members. Collect as many photos as you can.

CHAPTER 5:
SHARING WITH OTHER DETECTIVES

Family tree researchers are like a relay team in a track meet. The better they work together, the more likely they are to win a medal. In the same way, the more information genealogists share, the more likely they are to find out about their ancestors. They gladly share tips and bits of information and family trees with other researchers.

Before you can do much sharing with other family tree detectives, you have to do some organization. Computers can store most of the information, if that's the way you like to work. You can scan photos and other original documents. Almost all information can be saved on your hard drive or flash drive and made searchable. Just be sure to back up your work in case your computer crashes.

Even though it's possible to confine research to the computer, a great many family tree researchers don't do it that way. More often they have piles of paper, books, and photos stacked on their desks, shelves, and floors.

How do you handle the teetering piles that threaten to spill everywhere? It's ideal to organize your papers from the first day you print some census data or find a box of old photos in the attic.

Sort, sort, sort! Your system can be as simple as using a few boxes to divide material into categories. You might put old photos in one box, printed family information in another, and tips for research in another. Or you might use file folders and a filing cabinet to create a system to help you find things. Binders can be used to group information from different branches of your family tree.

Scrapbooks will hold photos and old letters. Be sure that any paper or plastic that touches an old photo or document is acid-free. Otherwise the ink on the documents will fade, as will the images on the photos. You may want to index photos so that you don't have to label them in any way. Do not label photos or documents on their front or back. You could put them in acid-free envelopes or other holders and label the holder.

Once you're organized, it's time to share your family tree information with others. Hopefully you will receive information in return. There are several ways to share.

Once again the computer takes the prize for being the best way to share with other family tree researchers. There are hundreds of genealogy web sites and blogs. A few, such as Ancestry.com, are for paying members, but many are free to everyone. In 1995, Cyndi Howell started a web site called Cyndi's List, which contains a huge database of genealogy web sites, blogs, and other useful information.

The biggest advantage to a paid site such as Ancestry.com is its size. With more people contributing information about family members, the chances of finding good information is made easier. Paid sites can also hire full-time researchers to digitize and index records, providing new information for their customers. However, no matter what site you use, there is no guarantee that the information provided by other members is correct. You will have to cross-check the information—but you'll have a good place to start.

There are also free genealogy web sites, including the USGenWeb Project and FamilySearch. Volunteers from all over the United States run the USGenWeb Project. The site provides links

The Mormon Family History Library in Salt Lake City, Utah, holds thousands of microfilmed birth and death records. They are kept in cabinets in long hallways. It is possible to borrow these microfilms or to look at them at the library.

to all state genealogy web sites, which in turn provide links to individual county information. These links are free.

FamilySearch is the product of one of the most famous family history sources. The Church of Jesus Christ of Latter-day Saints, known as the Mormon Church, has been collecting genealogical records for over a hundred years. Although kept for religious purposes, these records are also available for family tree research. The Mormon Family History Library in Salt Lake City, Utah, is the largest genealogical library in the world. The collection has information about more than two billion people, and access to records from more than 100 countries. All this information is being transferred to digital records.

These free web sites also have links to genealogy magazines and newsletters and offer fill-in-the-blank family history charts. You can fill in the blanks and print out your family tree. If you find a new ancestor next week, you can enter him or her and reprint the form.

So how would you find out if your great-great-great-great-uncle Sylvester rode up San Juan Hill with Teddy Roosevelt in the Spanish-American War? Since your grandma doubts that Sylvester was old enough to be a soldier in that war, a good first step would be to discover Sylvester's birth date. You could look for him in census rolls beginning in 1930, if that's still the last year available, and go back in time. If he was born after 1883, he wouldn't have been old enough to serve in the military in 1898. That would answer your question right away. If he was born before 1883, he might have been old enough—but that's just one clue.

Some census records, including the 1930 edition, tell whether or not a person served in the military and sometimes other information about that service. If you discover that Uncle Sylvester

British soldiers pose for a picture atop a captured German Panzer tank in the Middle East during World War II. Perhaps your great-grandfather was also a soldier in that war.

was a veteran, it will be on the military records.

Since you are looking for Uncle Sylvester along with Teddy Roosevelt, you could first look for Teddy Roosevelt's unit: the 1st U.S. Volunteer Cavalry, nicknamed the Rough Riders. Colonel Roosevelt led the Rough Riders on two charges up San Juan Hill in Cuba. You will likely be able to find a list of Rough Riders by searching the National Archives or other military records.

But there's another quirk—several other units joined the Rough Riders in the battle for San Juan Hill. That expands your search to find Uncle Sylvester. He might also have served with the 71st New York unit or the 1st South Carolina unit.[1] If your family has Latin American roots and came from Cuba, Uncle Sylvester might have served with the rebel Cuban forces.

Researching your family tree will always be a puzzle. What you find out may help you feel like part of a much bigger family than just your parents and grandparents.

You'll probably never be totally finished with research once you start. A new bit of information will pop up online and you'll say, "Ah-hah! So that's what happened." And you'll be off on a quest to find yet another piece of the puzzle that is your family tree.

Searching for a name on a search engine such as Google is always worth a try. Google Books, which is available by clicking the More tab at the top of the Google homepage, may turn up books or articles written by your ancestors or mentions of them in other writers' works.

CHAPTER NOTES

Chapter 1. Puzzling Out the Past
1. Ky Sha, "Understanding Genetics: Ask a Geneticist," The Tech Museum, Stanford School of Medicine, 2004. http://www.thetech. org/genetics/ask.php?id=29
2. Anahad O'Connor, "Really?" *The New York Times Health,* October 11, 2005. http://query.nytimes.com/gst/fullpage.html?res=9403EFDD 163FF932A25753C1A9639C8B63

Chapter 2. The Begats
1. S. Percy Smith, *Hawaiki: The Original Home of the Maori with a Sketch of Polynesian History* (London and Melbourne: Whitcomb and Tombs Limited, 1904), p. 20. http://www.nzetc.org/tm/scholarly/ tei-SmiHawa.html
2. Donna Potter-Phillips, "History of Genealogy," *Family Chronicle,* July/August 1999. http://www.familychronicle.com/ HistoryOfGenealogy.html
3. The National Heritage Museum, "Ellis Island," March 26, 2009. http://nationalheritagemuseum.typepad.com/library_and_archives/ ellis-island/

Chapter 3. Finding the First Clues
1. Christine Rose and Kay Germain Ingalls, *The Complete Idiot's Guide to Genealogy* (New York: Alpha Books, 2005), p. 287.

Chapter 4. Digging Deeper
1. Christine Rose and Kay Germain Ingalls, *The Complete Idiot's Guide to Genealogy* (New York: Alpha Books, 2005), p. 123.

Chapter 5. Sharing with Other Detectives
1. The Theodore Roosevelt Association, "The Rough Riders and Colonel Roosevelt," accessed September 29, 2010. http:// theodoreroosevelt.org/life/rough_riders.htm

FURTHER READING

BOOKS

Adolph, Anthony. *Who Am I? The Family Tree Explorer.* London, UK: Quercus Publishing, 2009.

Alexander, Keely, and Velani Mynhardt Witthoft. *Davy Brown Discovers His Roots.* Seattle: Big Tent Books & Keely Velani LLC, 2009.

Beller, Susan Provost. *Roots For Kids: A Genealogy Guide for Young People.* Baltimore: Genealogical Publishing Company, 2007.

Lee, Lonica. *My Family Tree.* Scoresby, Australia: The Five Mile Press, 2010.

Perl, Lila. *The Great Ancestor Hunt: The Fun of Finding Out Who You Are.* New York: Clarion, 1989.

WORKS CONSULTED

Adolph, Anthony. *Tracing Your Family History.* London: Collins, 2004.

Blake, Paul, and Maggie Loughran. *Discover Your Roots: Dig Up Your Family History and Other Buried Treasures.* New York: Perigee, 2006.

Kashuba, Melinda. *Walking With Your Ancestors: A Genealogist's Guide to Using Maps and Geography.* Cincinnati, OH: Family Tree Books, 2005.

Melnyk, Marcia Yannizze. *The Weekend Genealogist: Timesaving Techniques for Effective Research.* Cincinnati, OH: Betterway Books, 2000.

Morgan, George. *Genealogy.* New York: McGraw-Hill, 2009.

O'Connor, Anahad. "Really?" *The New York Times Health,* October 11, 2005. http://query.nytimes.com/gst/fullpage.html?res=9403EFDD163FF9 32A25753C1A9639C8B63

Potter-Phillips, Donna. "History of Genealogy." *Family Chronicle,* July/August 1999. http://www.familychronicle.com/HistoryOfGenealogy.html

Powell, Kimberly. *The Everything Family Tree Book: Research and Preserve Your Family History.* Avon, MA: Adams Media, 2006.

Robinson, Tara Rodden. *Genetics for Dummies.* Indianapolis: Wiley Publishing, Inc., 2005.

Rose, Christine, and Kay Germain Ingalls. *The Complete Idiot's Guide to Genealogy.* New York: Alpha Books, 2005.

Sha, Ky. "Understanding Genetics: Ask a Geneticist." The Tech Museum, Stanford School of Medicine, 2004. http://www.thetech.org/genetics/ask.php?id=29

Smith, S. Percy. *Hawaiki: The Original Home of the Maori with a Sketch of Polynesian History.* London and Melbourne: Whitcomb and Tombs Limited, 1904. http://www.nzetc.org/tm/scholarly/tei-SmiHawa.html

Smolenyak, Megan. *Who Do You Think You Are? The Essential Guide to Tracing Your Family History.* New York: Viking, 2009.

Sturdevant, Katherine Scott. *Organizing & Preserving Your Heirloom Documents.* Cincinnati, OH: Betterway Books, 2002.

FURTHER READING

ON THE INTERNET

Ancestry.com (fee site)
    http://www.ancestry.com
The Association of Professional Genealogists
    http://www.apgen.org/
The Board for Certification of Genealogists
    (Professional Genealogist Directory)
    http://www.bcgcertification.org/
Cyndi's List of Genealogy Sites on the Internet
    http://www.cyndislist.com
Dead Fred Genealogy Photo Archive
    http://www.deadfred.com
Family Search
    http://www.familysearch.org
Immigrant Ships Transcribers Guild
    http://immigrantships.net/
The National Archives: Resources for Genealogists and Family Historians
    http://archives.gov/genealogy/
The [UK] National Archives Learning Curve: Focus on the Domesday Book
    http://www.learningcurve.gov.uk/focuson/domesday
The National Heritage Museum
    http://www.nationalheritagemuseum.org/
Online Searchable Death Indexes & Records
    http://www.deathindexes.com/
Rootsweb.ancestry.com (free but associated with a fee site)
    http://www.rootsweb.ancestry.com
The Statue of Liberty–Ellis Island Foundation: Genealogy Learning Center
    http://www.ellisisland.org/genealogy/index.asp
Surname Database: Last Name Origins
    http://www.surnamedb.com/
The Theodore Roosevelt Association
    http://theodoreroosevelt.org/
The Trans-Atlantic Slave Trade Database
    http://www.slavevoyages.org/tast/index.faces
USGenWeb Project
    http://www.usgenweb.org/

GLOSSARY

ancestor (AN-ses-ter)—A person from whom another person is directly descended; a blood relative from a previous generation.

archive (AR-kyv)—A collection of records; also the place where these items are stored.

census (SEN-sus)—A count of people; the U.S. census is done every ten years.

data (DAH-tuh or DAY-tuh)—Information relating to a specific subject, such as a person's name, address, and date of birth.

descendant (dee-SEN-dent)—A person who is the offspring of a generation.

generation (jeh-nuh-RAY-shun)—A single stage of people who were born and living at the same time; a group of people that make up a single step between ancestors and descendants, usually defined as lasting thirty years.

immigrant (IH-muh-grunt)—A person who moves into a country or region from another one.

inherit (in-HAYR-it)—To receive land, money, or other possessions from an ancestor, usually at the time of the ancestor's death.

matrilineal (mat-rih-LIH-nee-ul)—Coming from the mother's side of the family.

obituary (oh-BIT-choo-ayr-ee)—An official announcement of a person's death, often with a description of his or her life.

patrilineal (pat-rih-LIH-nee-ul)—Coming from the father's side of the family.

surname (SUR-naym)—The family name or last name of a person.

INDEX

ABOUT THE AUTHOR

Bonnie Hinman is the author of 20 books for young people, including *We Visit Peru* and *The Massachusetts Bay Colony* for Mitchell Lane Publishers. Her biography of W.E.B. Du Bois, *A Stranger in My Own House*, published by Morgan Reynolds, was selected for inclusion on the 2006 New York Public Library's Books for the Teen Age. Hinman graduated from Missouri State University and lives in southwest Missouri with her husband, Bill, who is a great genealogy sleuth. Their children and four grandchildren live nearby.